Discipleship
with
James

Discipleship with James

Devotionals for
Spiritual Growth

Rick L. Upchurch

Tools To Lead Publishing
Huntington, IN

Dedicated to Mary Margaret

My wife, my best friend,

The best person I know.

Table of Contents

Introduction

We live in a postmodern age in which there are few, if any, absolutes; where every standard is up for grabs and the widely-touted "Family Values" mean different things to different groups. In this age, as throughout history, the Word of God brings clarity and stability. Many in our world regard the Bible as simply another book, yet for those who embrace the message within its pages, a tangible foundation emerges in the swirling mists of this uncertain time. That foundation is a relationship with God.

I believe all of life can be reduced to relationships. I suppose I'm a bit of a mystic. I believe the truths in the Bible give me a connecting point to the Divine. Beyond all human understanding, and thus plausibility, we are able to enter into relationship with God. For some, God is an antiquated concept, yet for those who have established that connection with God through the message, a new way of life emerges. This devotional, based on a section of the Bible, seeks to practically apply God's message for this age, and to make possible an ever-deepening relationship with both God and others.

The various narratives within this book are not intended to be comprehensive in interpretation. Rather, the intent is to present, through the tool of narrative thought, insight into how the truth in the book of James relates to everyday life. This volume may be used as a commentary to provide insight on a particular passage, as the starting point for a discussion in a small group setting, or read as a personal devotional. It is my hope that these thoughts will comfort, inform, inspire, and challenge the reader.

Bonus Retreat Section:

At the end of this book there is a separate section which can be used in a retreat format, either alone or with a small group of trusted friends. By retreat I mean separating yourself away from the distractions of your normal life for three to five hours. Taking this time once a month can have a powerful effect on your ability to navigate the challenges faced each day. Simply follow the directions and enjoy your time with God.

Day 1 - Trials, Troubles, and Attitude

"Consider it pure joy, my brothers..."

James 1:2

There are many examples of "pure joy." Here are a few:

- Hearing about the birth of a baby.

- Cresting the highest point of a roller coaster.

- Enjoying a piece of hot blackberry pie with vanilla ice cream melting all over the top.

- Watching a beautiful sunset hand-in-hand with my wife.

- Holding my children when they

were babies as they lay sleeping on my lap.

- Hearing the testimony of someone who has found the hope and peace available to those who accept Jesus as Lord.

However, the whole verse in James 1 contains more than joy. The full verse reads: "Consider it pure joy, my brothers, whenever you face trials of many kinds, because you know that the testing of your faith develops perseverance." Now, I must confess, "pure joy" is not what immediately leaps to my mind in the face of trials. Trials typically involve some kind of pain. That pain may be financial, physical, emotional, mental, etc.

Whatever form the pain comes in, it is still pain, and personally, I have a hard time equating pain with "pure joy."

So, do we determine in the very beginning that James is one of those people who have never really had bad things happen to him and glibly goes through life telling everyone else that they should be like him, or is there a deeper message here? The answer may lie in the goal, i.e. the development of perseverance.

I am reminded of Romans 8:28 in which we are assured "...that all things work together for the good of those who love God and are called according to His purpose." Paul also writes in Philippians 3:13b-14 "Forgetting what is behind and straining toward what is ahead, I press on toward the goal...." In other words, the reality of *NOW* is a building block toward a future. *We are able to choose our future by how we build the blocks together.* If our perspective is faith and hope, we will build a bright future with Christ with blocks of joy and anticipation; if our perspective is selfishness and anger, we build a dungeon with thick bars with blocks of hopelessness and despair.

A fire once swept through a forest destroying the trees that had taken several lifetimes to grow. As the old forest ranger walked through the charred remains, he began to see the saplings springing up where their great ancestors had once stood. So it is in our lives; each day brings the possibility of hope and life in the midst of pain. We make the choice of how we perceive our reality.

Have you ever felt helpless in the face of the circumstances in your life? On a piece of paper or in a personal journal, list some of those circumstances. Beside each item, mark whether or not it developed a greater perseverance in your faith. Then describe how you might be able to make this trial a building block for the future.

"Counting it pure joy" is a developed ability. We are not born with it and it will require the exercise of spiritual muscles, and will include all the soreness that accompanies exercising our physical muscles.

Day 2 - Relationships and Perseverance

"Because you know that the testing of your faith develops perseverance. Perseverance must finish its work so that you may be mature and complete, not lacking anything."

James 1:3-4

Perseverance is one of those words that most of us would just as soon eliminate from our vocabulary. The mere thought of persevering brings to mind toil and misery. Sometimes, persevering means "to just hold on" through the monotony of everyday life. The key, of course, is to hold on during the misery or boredom. The singing group Wilson Philips in a song titled "Hold On" sing in the chorus:

"Don't you know, things can change, Things'll go your way, If you hold on for just one more day." Maybe that is part of the secret—to take one day at a time.

For the Christian, however, there is more to it than that. I know a little bit about going through hard times, and I have discovered three principles that have helped me persevere and, I think, become more mature.

First, perseverance is directly proportional to our willingness to lean fully on Jesus. Leaning on Jesus means to cry unto the Lord with the weight of your pain. Refusing to endure in stoic silence, I take my burden to Jesus in prayer; not just a quick prayer while working out the problem on my own, but a focused outpouring of my heart. Jesus often drew apart from his disciples to lean on His Father. Job, a character from the Old Testament book by the same name, is a supreme example of suffering. He spent a great deal of time in prayer and dialogue with the Lord. As He did for Job, Jesus cares about our problems and stands ready to support us through our struggles with His presence.

Second, share your hurts and disappointments with a friend. The support of another person who genuinely cares for you can provide great comfort and emotional support. Often, our natural tendency is to keep our problems to ourselves and, thus, lose this great aid. Be open enough with a close friend to share your hurts and you will find the road of your life a little easier to travel. This may be more difficult for some than others. Here are some considerations in finding someone who you trust to help carry your burdens:

1. That person should be a mature Christian.

2. That person should be someone who knows how to keep a confidence.

It has been my experience that often the mere act of sharing a problem or concern with another person has a liberating effect. Saying the words out loud often robs the problem of its power to dominate your life.

Finally, remember what Paul said to the Christians at Corinth, "God is faithful, he will not let you be tempted beyond what you can bear. But when you are tempted, he will also provide a way out so that you can stand up under it." (1 Corinthians 10:13b), "I will not leave you nor forsake you, nor will I allow you to be tempted above your ability to bear-up." This is the light at the end of the tunnel.

Weary Christian, do not lose hope! Jesus is standing by, ready to cradle you in His arms and comfort you in the midst of your storm. Now is not the time to despair, but to lean on the Savior.

Day 3 - Asking...

"If any of you lacks wisdom, he should ask God, who gives generously to all without finding fault, and it will be given to him. But when he asks, he must believe and not doubt."

James 1:5-6a

This verse really speaks to me, "If any of you lacks wisdom..." Yep, that about describes me!

With wisdom we can avoid various problems in life and take advantage of many opportunities. With wisdom we can know when to share our faith with others and know when to keep quiet. With wisdom we can walk into difficult situations and come out unscathed. Wisdom is one of the keys to a satisfying life.

There are areas of my life where I desperately need wisdom. One of those areas is rearing my children; another is determining just what I need to do as a husband to fulfill my wife's needs; and still another is how to guide my teenagers to make godly decisions. As you can imagine, the list can get quite endless.

Take raising children, for instance. I want to raise my children to know of God's love, and it is my utmost desire to see them accept Him as their Savior. But, how do I go about that? I have seen wonderful Christian couples whose children turn completely away from God, and others whose children grow up loving the Lord and serving Him with all their hearts.

What makes the difference? I know there is a personal decision on the part of the child somewhere in all this, but I really need wisdom to get my part right! I don't want to wait around for time to bring me wisdom, nor do I want to make mistakes to gain wisdom (even though I have made many and will probably make many more!). In this text, I find that I can obtain wisdom simply by asking and believing. God's Word offers this promise, if I am wise enough to grab hold and build it into my life. So, I find myself praying for wisdom when I face decisions, when I get into difficult situations all the time and I have discovered the promise to be true. God *does* provide wisdom—

His wisdom—in the face of our need, if we only ask and believe.

Dear God, help me be wise. Help me to display love instead of bitterness or indifference. Help me to heal wounds instead of opening them, Please, God may you grant me wisdom — Amen.

Day 4 - Two-Face

"...He who doubts is like a wave of the sea, blown and tossed by the wind. That man should not think he will receive anything from the Lord; he is a double-minded man, unstable in all he does."

James 1:6b-8

The concept of double-mindedness might be more easily understood using the term "two-faced." Two-faced is defined as presenting one "face" (attitude, philosophy, or belief) in one situation, and presenting a different "face" when in another situation. One of the most common example of being two-faced can be found in certain political figures seeking election. They promise one thing to one group, and the opposite to another. In the Christian realm, the double-minded man has had some high visibility in certain TV evangelists who proclaim their faith publicly, yet live contrary to scriptural teachings. Another word for this type of person is: "hypocrite."

So, how does being double-minded (two-faced) connect to doubting? Pierce through the shell we build around ourselves and get to the core of who we are—I think it lies directly at that point, deep within a person. Who are you, really? Do you know what you believe? Do you know the values that guide your life? As Christians, we have declared Jesus to be Lord in our lives. This is what we say, but when we live contrary to Christianity principles there is conflict within us. Our lives do not match our words, and our core values are out of sync with our behavior. It's surprising how often those who live this dual life do not even recognize the disconnect; they attend church, pray daily, give faithfully, and yet cheat on their taxes, abuse their children, are unfaithful to their spouses, etc. and wonder why God is not blessing their lives.

This is not the doubting of genuine inquiry, but the hypocrisy of one whose double-mindedness is the result of wanting "to have the cake and eat it too;" to say "I am a Christian," yet live with no regard for the lifestyle demands of that faith.

Here are some ways to keep from being counted in this group:

1. Identify your core values: What do you believe? Why? If you truly believed, how would you have to change your behavior?

2. Be slow to speak: The old adage of "being silent and thought as possibly a fool, as opposed to opening your mouth and removing all doubt" seems to apply here. When you speak without careful thought behind your words you may make promises that can't be kept, or make statements that aren't true.

3. Tell the truth: The temptation is often to say what you believe your

audience wants to hear. If truth is your practice you can avoid getting caught in a lie, no matter how well meant, which will undermine your credibility and influence.

4. Realize you may have to take an unpopular stance. When my children were young, our core values dictated that 'R' rated movies contained language and behavior that were unacceptable to watch in our home. This limitation was not popular, but it was consistent with our faith and values, and I believe modeled something important to our children about being single-minded.

Day 5 - Ants and Rubber Tree Plants

"Blessed is the man who perseveres under trial, because when he has stood the test, he will receive the Crown of Life that God has promised to those who love Him."

James 1:12

When I read this passage, the picture that comes to mind is a scene from the old TV show "Laverne & Shirley." On more than one occasion, Laverne had given up on a situation only to have Shirley start singing that little song about an ant moving a rubber tree plant.

Next time you're found,

with your chin on the ground

There a lot to be learned, so look around

Just what makes that little old ant
Think he'll move that rubber tree plant
Anyone knows an ant, can't
Move a rubber tree plant.

But he's got high hopes, he's got high hopes
He's got high apple pie, in the sky hopes

So any time you're gettin' low
'stead of lettin' go
Just remember that ant
Oops there goes another rubber tree plant.
Writer(s): Cahn/Van Heusen

The more she sings, the brighter Laverne's mood gets, until once again, they are off attempting the absurd, if not the impossible. Now, "everyone knows an ant can't move a rubber tree plant," but high hopes keep him trying. I don't know what an ant hopes for, but I find what I am supposed to hope for clearly spelled out in this verse: "The Crown of Life." Wow! I have lived just long enough to figure out that trials are going to come and go, whether I am a Christian or not. But these trials are easier to bear when I remember Christ is my personal Savior, and that He will never allow me to go through more than I can handle (1 Corinthians 10:13).

This admonition to persevere is a reminder from God. "Hang in there," Jesus says, "sure you are going through trials now, but there will come a day when, because you have been faithful, you will receive the reward, eternal life in the heavenly realms." (c.f. Matthew 16:27)

God has promised us this very special reward; sometimes that is all that keeps me working at my "rubber tree plant." Our Lord warned us about this ahead of time, saying: "In this world, you *will* have trouble, but take heart! I have overcome the world!" (John 16:33)   I have high hopes based on the Word of God and the saving power of the blood of Jesus Christ, my wonderful Lord. I know, with God's help, I *can* move that rubber tree plant . . . and you can too!

Day 6 - Postmoderns aren't tempted, are they?

"When tempted, no one should say, 'God is tempting me.' For God cannot be tempted by evil, nor does he tempt anyone; but each one is tempted when, by his own evil desire, he is dragged away and enticed. Then, after desire has conceived, it gives birth to sin; and sin, when it is full-grown gives birth to death."

James 1:13-15

Wow! James sure has a way with words doesn't he? I have felt the same way before; you know, that God is tempting me, trying to see just how far I will go before I fall flat on my face, which usually isn't too far. But James says that God doesn't tempt anyone. In fact, another passage (I Corinthians 10:13) supports that statement and adds: "No temptation has seized you except what is common to man. And God is faithful. He will not let you be tempted beyond what you can bear. But when you are tempted, he will also provide a way out so that you can stand up under it." I don't know about you, but I have that verse underlined in my Bible and memorized.

But, if it is not God tempting us, it must be Satan, and since we all know how powerful Satan is, there is obviously no chance that I could win the battle anyway so...HOLD ON! Let us not give Satan too much power! After all, in I Corinthians 10:13, God promises us a way to escape the devil's schemes. According to James, the primary reason we fall is not because "the devil made me do it;" our own desires are the culprit. That brings me to the two basic keys to staying out of the mess described in James 1:15—namely, "death."

The first key is to take a good look at your head! The head has three crucial senses that enable the body to function: hearing, seeing, and speaking (remember the three monkeys: Hear No Evil, See No Evil, and Speak No Evil?). If we are going to avoid death, it is absolutely necessary that we bring our head to God! What comes in through the ears and eyes has the ability to draw our attention away from God, and establish that destructive cycle mentioned in James. It's a domino-effect: if you insist on listening to dirty jokes or negative gossip, or looking at pornographic paraphernalia and filth, you will begin to crave more and more of it! These things are just as addictive to the sinful nature as alcohol and drugs. They will lure you further and further away from God until your soul is totally separate from Christ—and "life." And I haven't even mentioned your brain and what you think about, but that is part of the head, and you can be sure whatever occupies your thought life also affects whether you stand or fall. If you want to be victorious, take a good, long look at your head; if what you see there bothers you; take it to Jesus in prayer. Ask Him to help you clean it up.

The second key is to take a good look at your heart! In other words, what is the focus of your life? Where are you headed? What is important to you? Problems come when the focus of our lives is on anything other than Christ. Now I know this takes a little work, (at least it has for me) but once Jesus and His Will become the focus of your heart, you will begin to see a new dimension of God's blessing and mighty power working in your life. Instead of shuffling along, terrified of stumbling and falling, you can march in time to the call of the Savior—HEAVENWARD!

Just remember this: "God does not tempt us—we do," and to overcome these temptations:

1. Take a good look at your head (garbage in or garbage out).
2. Take a good look at your heart (what do you want most?).

Day 7 – What's the Name of the Game?

"Don't be deceived my dear brothers. Every good and perfect gift is from above, coming down from the Father of the heavenly lights, who does not change like shifting shadows. He chose to give us birth through the Word of Truth, that we might be a kind of first fruits of all He created."

James 1:16-18

"Don't be deceived," James writes, and I want to say "Ha!" Deception seems to be the name of the game. I don't know what it was like then, but now, it seems everyone has their own version of the truth. So, which one do you believe? Which one is true?

If I'm going to avoid deception, I'm going to have to know the details, all the details, and have enough wisdom and competence to make an informed decision. Let me give you an example. Have you ever applied for a credit card? The form you sign if filled with small print which they count on you not reading. However, if you don't pay attention to the details, you may end up paying high interest charges and large annual fees.

The alternative to knowing all the details, and having the wisdom and competence to interpret them, is trust. You can trust the credit card company to look after itself and its profits. Thus, you can gauge "trust-ability" by motive. The credit card company's motive is its profit, but what is God's motive? Scripture keeps coming back to the theme that God's motive is love, genuine love, for us. That was the motive for Jesus' sacrifice on the cross, after all, what else was gained except the possibility of salvation and new birth for us?

James says, "Don't be deceived," don't buy into a philosophy that our lives are governed by fate and coincidence. Don't let new-age spirituality persuade you that crystals, spells, positive self-talk, or good thoughts are the source of good in your life. No matter how far you may have strayed from God's will, you can have confidence in this: God loves you and wants the best for you.

Day 8 - Good and Bad

"Don't be deceived, my brothers. Every good and perfect gift is from above, coming down from the Father of heavenly lights, who does not change like shifting shadows. He chose to give us birth through the Word of truth, that we might be a kind of first fruits of all he created."

James 1:16-18

Here James reminds us that God is the author of all the good that comes into our lives. The most important of those "good gifts" is the gift of new birth. The acceptance of Christ as personal Savior, the forgiveness of sins, turning away from sin, these are all truly good gifts. I marvel at the number of people I see who either do not know of these good gifts, or have forgotten what theses gift can accomplish.

I was talking to someone recently who, after asking what time the services were at the church I attended, made the statement, "I know I'm a sinner and don't need anyone telling me where I'm headed." How very sad it is when someone realizes his eternal destination, yet for whatever reason, chooses to remain on that path to utter destruction and eternal suffering.

I saw in a local newspaper that child abuse and molestation has more than doubled in the past eight years. I see people in the hospital whose lives are permanently damaged due to the effects of alcohol and drug dependency. My heart longs to ask, "Do you know about God's good gifts?" Yet, more often than not, the shifting shadows of their world make them suspicious of a Father who truly loves them, and is the same loving God today, tomorrow, and forever. Good gifts are suspicious to those who have only known fighting, hatred, despair, and poverty. That there can be no good gifts is a lie that Satan will continue to spread in his attempts to deceive this unsuspecting world in which we live. Indeed, he is very successful, for even those good gifts given by our Father are occasionally forgotten by those who have tasted God's goodness and have later been deceived by Satan's deception.

Our world is in constant need of those who can give away the gift of Love—those willing to let their friends and relatives (and everyone else) in on the goodness that has been freely given to them. Many churches are reaching out with that good gift and lives are being brought from the shadows into the light; but there is still much to be done. As Christians, must continue to be light and love to a cold, dark age. I encourage you, brothers and sisters, do not be deceived. Your love and concern are more important now than ever in bringing light into before in helping Jesus beat back the darkness and the shadows of this dying world. Keep on keeping on!

Day 9 - Listen, Did You Hear That?

"Everyone should be quick to listen, slow to speak, and slow to become angry. For man's anger does not bring about the righteous life that God desires for him. Therefore, get rid of all moral filth and the evil that is so prevalent, and humbly accept the Word planted in you, which can save you."

James 1:19-21

This may very well be the hardest commandment found in God's Word. Quick to listen, slow to speak, and slow to become angry? My inclination is to finish sentences for whomever I am talking to, just so that I can start talking. Slow to speak? That's a toughie. Maybe the secret to understanding how to be slow to speak and slow to become angry lies in the first part: quick to listen. Listening, not merely hearing the word, but actually listening, seems to be a lost art in our day.

What does it mean to listen to someone? I think it means to hear their hurt, to hear the emotions they are feeling, to be able to internalize a little bit of where they are at, and what they are going through. To identify with Paul when he says to "think of others more highly than yourself" would be to listen to their life. Maybe that would make it easier to be slow to speak.

I know this is something that takes a great deal of effort and practice to make a reality. You don't automatically walk out your door and say, "Well, today I'm going to be quick to listen and slow to speak" and have it happen that easily. In some conversations, it seems to work out naturally—you listen, you hear, and then respond. Other situations don't go so smoothly, particularly when there is stress in your life, which has a way of bubbling up to the surface. I think James is really into discipline, and this is one of the disciplines that will benefit our lives, but is so hard to put into effect. How do you do it? The same way you start any discipline in your life—one day at a time; one conversation at a time.

The whole concept of being slow to anger is one that would strengthen each of us. Anger almost always produces an emotional storm within a person. The expression of that anger (if you can express it, leave it, and walk away in forgiveness), is not always bad. But in order to be slow to anger, we must learn to disassociate ourselves personally from the issues being discussed. That sounds easy, doesn't it? To disassociate one's self is to remove my feelings from the issues, and decide which issues are important enough to fight about, which issues are negotiable, and which ones aren't even important.

Ed Friedman, a noted counselor calls this "responding with a non-anxious presence." I get the feeling that many people will fight about almost anything! Even things that, in the grand scheme of things, are totally unimportant, just because they are *our* opinions and our opinions have to be right! I find myself falling prey to that from time-to-time. It is always good when an opinion (or a fight or an argument) arises, to stop and say, "Is this really that important? So what if the car is blue-ish green or green-ish blue! Really, does it make that much difference?" Many things seem important because we haven't established what *is* important in life—a relationship with Jesus Christ. We allow a lot of little things to become a major issue because we want to avoid a commitment to a major thing. It's something to think about isn't it

Day 10 - There IS Information Available

"Do not merely listen to the Word, and so deceive yourselves. Do what it says. Anyone who listens to the Word but does not do what it says is like a man who looks at his face in the mirror and after looking at himself, goes away and immediately forgets what he looks like. But the man who looks intently into the perfect law that gives freedom and continues to do this, not forgetting what he has heard but doing it—he will be blessed in what he does."

James 1:22-25

I am constantly amazed that there is real power available in the Word of God. Pardon me for being a bit mystical, but, first, I have found that the Word of God is anointed with the power of God and that by merely reading it aloud, there is made available power to accomplish miraculous works in the name of Christ. Perhaps even more important for the average person is the presence of the power for every day victorious living, which brings me to the second amazing thing.

If we are going to call ourselves Christians and tap into the fullness of God's power for victorious daily living, we are going to have to expose ourselves to the Word. Listen to what James says, "Do not merely listen to the Word...Do what it says." Action, based on the Word, is the hallmark of the true believer. While power is made available in the reading of the Word, it falls to the ground and is gone unless we are willing to do what it says. Reading is good, doing is even better.

Are you a doer of the Word, or do you look for things with which you can easily agree and, perhaps, do those, while ignoring the rest. "I don't have any money to give so I'll just ignore the portions of Scripture that refer to faithful giving." "The Pastor hurt my feelings the other Sunday so I'm going to skip those passages on forgiveness." We are happy to treat the Word like a lottery, letting it fall open to select verses for specific needs but ignoring the fact that it was meant to be the basis of our relationship with Christ. How can you *do* what it says if you do not *know* what it says?

Day 11 - Nobody is Going to Tell Me What I Cannot Say!

"If anyone considers himself religious and yet does not keep a tight reign on his tongue, he deceives himself and his religion is worthless. Religion that God our Father accepts as pure and faultless is this: to look after orphans and widows in their distress and to keep oneself from being polluted by the world."

James 1:26-27

This seems like common sense, doesn't it? After all, how could James possibly expect anyone to take him seriously? If you were to believe James, you would actually have to make a connection between what is said and whether or not our religion is worth anything. What a joke! I mean, isn't there such a thing as freedom of speech in this country? I know my rights; nobody can tell me what I can say or cannot say. Who does James think he is anyway? Why, just the other day I heard the most interesting bit of news, and someone has to pass these things on, don't they? Personally, I think it is pretty extreme for anyone to take what James says here seriously. I have heard of "loose lips sink ships," but he is trying to say that loose lips indicate a *disease of the soul,* which invalidates my faith in God?

Doesn't he understand how hard it is to reign in my tongue once I get started? Surely he isn't opposed to a little Christian fellowship and conversation, and if I were to worry about pollution, I might miss some really interesting TV. Okay, so when you watch TV, you have to strain out some pollution. You know, things like language unfit for Christians, extra-marital sex, and other influences that prompt us to sin. If we were to avoid all these pollutants, we probably would not get to watch much TV at all, and then what would we do with our time?

I think this James guy must be a radical. The church doesn't need radicals! Look at Jesus, He was a radical and look what it got Him!...Um...I wonder...

Day 12 - Are You in the Right Clique?

"My brothers, and believers in our glorious Lord Jesus Christ, don't show favoritism."

James 2:1

So starts a powerful section in James on who gets our time and attention. Again, the Word of God proves itself to be current. One church where I served as pastor was growing and lives were being changed. One day one of the leaders of the congregation pulled me aside and told me that the "new" people were not "their kind" of people. At another church the same situation arose and again someone spoke to me saying, "they just don't fit in." In one congregation it was because the new people were of a slightly lower socio-economic group (you know, they made less money), in the other congregation it was because the new people "dressed too nice." As I listened to these comments, my mind was drawn to this passage and the difficulty we, as humans, seem to have in accepting people who are different.

I suppose that is how cliques get started. Webster defines a clique as "a small, exclusive circle of people." Now I know that church cliques are never, well almost never, intentionally exclusive, but that does not necessarily mean they are inclusive either. Cliques, at their worst, exclude anyone who does not match their specific criteria for admission.

Often that criteria is an understood list of qualifications that might be difficult to put into words (i.e. "my group consists of those who kept this church alive during the hard times and why should these Johnny-Come-Latelys benefit from all our hard work.") When and if a clique develops, it is pretty obvious to everyone whether or not it is inclusive or exclusive by how the members of the clique include or exclude others. Sadly, those involved in cliques rationalize their prejudice and judgmental attitudes in a way which exonerates the exclusivity of the clique.

Some will say, "Well, we will include anyone who asks," yet make no intentional efforts to include anyone.

These groups (the accepted term for cliques) have acceptance criteria which only they know and, even then usually only subconsciously.

Prejudice, we all agree, is wrong and abhorrent in God's eyes. Yet James says in verse 9, "But if you show favoritism, you sin and are convicted by the law as lawbreakers." Of course, what he is saying from the reverse angle is that Christians are a people who should be controlled by love and acceptance without consideration of money, race, or clothing. Have you checked your pulse lately? Does your blood pool in favoritism and judgment or pulse with the warmth of God's love and acceptance? Break open your clique by intentionally reaching out

and including others; by doing so you
fulfill the law of love.

Day 13 – No-Limit Mercy

"Speak and act as those who are going to be judged by the law that gives freedom, because judgment without mercy will be shown to anyone who has not been merciful. Mercy triumphs over judgment."

James 2:12-13

Judgment! What a fear-inspiring word. It seems there is always someone around who is quick to judge everything we say or do, or, for that matter, *do not* say or *do not* do. It is easy to fall into a mindset where it feels as if everyone is judging you for something. What makes it worse is that at least some of the judgments are actually on target, meaning we now have to deal with guilt and inadequacy as well.

Sounds pretty hopeless, doesn't it? That is exactly the picture Satan wants us to get in our minds—that everyone is out to get everyone else and you better look out for yourself because no one else will. He is constantly at work devising strategies to make hopelessness the norm, and guilt the accepted way of life.

What Satan does not want us to discover is the full extent of God's mercy. How far does His mercy go? For the believer who truly wants God's will for His life, there are no limits to His mercy and forgiveness. That is why it says "mercy triumphs over judgment." No matter who is judging, or how bad the judging gets, the one who follows Christ has a friend and an intercessor in Jesus.

But there is more. This passage not only offers hope for you in the face of Satan's lies, but also contains a course of action for your life. Basically, that action is to be merciful toward others. You know, the old "do unto others as you would have them do unto you" rule. The reality is that all relationships, even our relationship with God, is affected by how seriously we take this rule. That is why James starts the passage with "See and act as those who are going to be judged." It is always a good idea to keep in mind that who we *are*, and what we *say* and *do* affects more than just ourselves.

The lesson here, then, is be merciful so that you will receive mercy; or cut the other person a little slack and it will come back to you; or do unto others as you would have them do unto you. Words to live by!

Day 14 – The Best Argument Against Christianity Is Christians

"What good is it, my brothers, if a man claims to have faith but has no deeds? Can such faith save him?

Suppose a brother or sister is without clothes and daily food. If one of you says to him, 'Go, I wish you well; keep warm and well fed,' but does nothing about his physical needs, what good is it? In the same way, faith by itself, if it is not accompanied by action, is dead. But someone will say, 'You have faith; I have deeds.' Show me your faith without deeds, and I will show you my faith by what I do. You believe that there is one God. Good! Even the demons believe that—and shudder. You foolish man, do you want evidence that faith without deeds is useless? Was not our ancestor

Abraham considered righteous for what he did when he offered his son Isaac on the altar? You see that his faith and his actions were working together, and his faith was made complete by what he did. And the scripture was fulfilled that says, 'Abraham believed God, and it was credited to him as righteousness,' and he was called God's friend. You see that a person is justified by what he does and not by faith alone."

James 2:14-24

Did you catch that last part—where it says, "... a person is justified by what he does and not by faith alone?" Some seek to be justified through their good works, others insist that justification is solely by faith. James clearly believes there has to be a balance. Must I really take the time out of *my* busy schedule to do something so mundane as 'good works'?" I am glad you asked. Several passages (I will only cite three here) point to that very obligation in support of what James says:

I Thessalonians 3:13 *"...never tire of doing right."*

I Timothy 6:18 *"Command them to do good, to be rich in good deeds, and to be generous and willing to share."*

I Timothy 5:25 *"In the same way good deeds are obvious..."*

Holiness, the Spirit-filled life, is a life of good works done in Jesus' name with the intent of bringing honor to Him. The Word says that those who believe and are filled with the Spirit are to make a difference in their world. If, somehow, Christians are not having a positive influence in our homes, schools, communities, workplaces, government, and local congregation—wherever we come in contact with the world—then there at least must be the suspicion that our claim to Christianity is self-deception at best, or an outright lie at worst.

Holiness is a verb. The Spirit-filled life is not a philosophical belief as much as a lifestyle. The power of the cross is the power for a changed life that sees others' needs and responds. Too many who call who call themselves Christians know little of what it truly means to be in Him. I once attended a conference where pastors and church leaders from a major city had gathered. While there, I witnessed an exchange between one of those leaders and a lady taking orders for the material being promoted. I was shocked as I heard the dignified, well-dressed church leader respond with rude speech and an obnoxious attitude. We are the Highway of Holiness for the world. It is our lives, our service, our positive impact that points to Christ, or validates the world's opinion that Christianity is a hoax and Christians are hypocrites.

Sheldon Vanavken writes: "The best argument for Christianity is Christians: their joy, their certainty, their completeness. But the strongest argument against Christianity is also Christians— when they are somber and joyless, when they are self-righteous and smug in complacent consecration, when they are narrow and repressive, then Christianity dies a thousand deaths."

Forget your schedule. Forget your personal preferences. What are you doing to bring glory to God? In what ways are you being the Highway of Holiness to the world in which you live? Are you a road sign pointing toward the narrow gate of life, or merely part of the herd heading to a horrendous hell?

Day 15 – Step-by-Step

"We all stumble in many ways. If anyone is never at fault in what he says, he is a perfect man, able to keep his whole body in check."

James 3:2

Knowing myself as I do, I like what James has to say here: "We all stumble and fall." No, I'm not supporting the thought that we sin every day in thought, word, and deed. Truthfully, I see no support for such a concept in Scripture. However, I know myself well enough to know that I am not above making mistakes or even stumbling a little in my walk. Too much of Christianity has removed the reality of our humanity and left us with the impression that only the perfect have the right to be called Christian.

If Christianity is anything, it is a process. It is a step-by-step, or stumble-by-stumble growing experience through which we become more like Christ. I am fully aware of the cleansing nature of the Holy Spirit and praise God for sanctification; yet, too many have assumed that such a filling compresses the totality of spiritual development and they never grow beyond that initial filling. Others, unfortunately, experience the filling and are dismayed, depressed, or defeated when they find that "we all stumble in many ways."

Someone wise once said that you cannot fail as long as you are trying. Translated, that means *never give up.*

Even though you may stumble, it is not because you are a failure, but because you are human. Keep on keeping on!

Day 16 - Full Speed Ahead!

"Who is wise and understanding among you? Let him show it by his good life, by deeds done in humility that comes from wisdom."

James 3:13

There seems to be a lot more talk about being wise today than there is actual wisdom. James makes a clear statement here which echoes the old adage, "the proof is in the pudding." It is one thing to talk of wisdom and deeds, but it is another to actually live wisely. James says the wise man will show it by his good life. The good life he was referring to breaks down pretty simply into two parts.

First, the wise man will cast off

the chains of sin and through true repentance, accept Jesus as Lord. The writer of the book of Proverbs writes that the beginning of wisdom is the fear of the Lord. His emphasis was that we never become wise until we perceive the awesomeness of God. A true look at God and the sacrifice of Jesus for our salvation leaves a clear choice for the wise person. When it becomes clear there is only one way to achieve salvation and that is through Jesus (Acts 4:12), then it is foolishness to attempt salvation through any other means.

Many are trapped in cults that offer only a portion of the truth. Foolishness and pride have caused the leaders to proclaim a salvation that does not have Jesus as the foundation. The result is a multitude of those who think they are wise while traveling full speed toward judgment. The wise person turns from sin or any other doctrine and places Jesus first.

Second, the wise person will have a lifestyle that reflects wisdom. Some things are obvious: those things that are harmful to the body and or mental processes should be avoided. Our bodies are not merely a collection of bones and muscles, but a residing place for the Spirit of God, if we have confessed Jesus as Savior. Living a good life, then, means avoiding those influences that harm the body. However, it goes beyond that. The good life is a life that is controlled by the law of love, love that comes from God redirects our vision to see each other and the world differently.

Through the eyes of love our response is to become involved in solutions for our life and our world. That means investing time, energy, and money in someone else. Like taking a Saturday to help re-roof a widow's house who cannot afford to have it done, or helping someone make much needed repairs on a vehicle. The good life James is talking about is not focused on *me* and *my* comfort but on making a difference for others in Jesus' name. He then goes on to include a little statement that in effect says, "No bragging." After all, God knows what you have done and He is the One who really counts.

So, the question is, "How wise are you?" If you have not acknowledged Jesus as Savior, then the answer, unfortunately, is not very wise. If you have accepted Him as your Savior, then how are you living? Are you a liver of the good life? Do you wisely invest in others as an expression of love, or focus totally on yourself? Think about what James has to say, and give it a try. I believe you will find being wise has its own rewards.

Day 17 - I'm Not the One Who Started It

"What causes fights and quarrels among you? Don't they come from your desires that battle within you? You want something but don't get it. You kill and covet, but you cannot have what you want. You quarrel and fight. You do not have, because you do not ask God. When you ask, you do not receive, because you ask with the wrong motives, so that you may spend what you get on your pleasures."

James 4:1-3

Boy, James has finally lost it! He has definitely gone too far. Where does he get off saying things like that? The reason I have quarrels is because of two things, and neither of them have to do with me. First, people do not understand me. Nobody ever tries to see things from my point-of-view. I cannot believe how many selfish people I know! Everybody always thinks they know best and nobody listens to me. If I have quarrels it is because I'm not willing to let anybody boss me around! Why can't they make a better effort at getting along with me? After all, I don't want to quarrel; they are the ones who just won't stop. *See, it's not my fault.*

Second, if I do quarrel, (and I don't quarrel unless someone else forces me to) it has nothing to do with what I receive or don't receive from God. But, since we're on that subject, I don't ask with wrong motives: ever, really! I think it would glorify God if He gave me a new convertible—it's not really for me, it's to let others see the goodness of God. Now how could James even imply that's somehow selfish? What I don't understand is why I haven't gotten the convertible and several other little things like that! I'm a child of God. I deserve a few nice things! Now James comes along and implies I'm selfish. Well, I can tell him a thing or two! If that's how this Christianity business works, I'm not interested. If God will not meet a few simple requests then He can do without me—see how far the church will get without me!

So goes the devotions of a person who has missed the point, lost sight of the goal. It's not about *our* rights or what *we* get, but what He gave—His blood. "For God so loved the world..."

Day 18 - Who Are Your Friends?

"You adulterous people, don't you know that friendship with the world is hatred toward God? Anyone who chooses to be friend of the world becomes an enemy of God."

James 4:4

Harsh words! Like a line drawn in the sand, James is attempting to make it perfectly clear who is on the Lord's side. Yet, there is some confusion. What does it mean to be a friend of the world? Is James saying that if I have friends who are non-Christians I am an enemy of God? Is he saying that if I go bowling, watch television, or listen to the radio, that I hate Him? What started out as a simple line has become a mountain that looms forbidding against the sky.

Christians are confused about their role in the world. Non-Christians see a mountain of expectations and are either intimidated by it and/or ridicule the absurdity of even attempting.

Part of the confusion lies squarely at the feet of well-meaning preachers and churches. With every intention of doing good, rules and standards have been handed out to *define* "Christian" behavior. With each rule, the mountain has grown and the path has become more obscure.

The bottom line is this: Have you confessed Jesus as Lord of your life AND do you honor Him as LORD of every part of your life?

Friendship with God means I put God first in my decisions, relationships, etc. It is not complicated. I take Jesus with me bowling, watching TV, and even listening to the radio. In fact, I take Jesus with me everywhere, because He is my friend. I don't like some of the things I used to, I don't watch some programs, I don't listen to some songs because of that friendship. There are even some of my old friends I don't hang with much anymore. Sometimes I miss them, but I know what I've got going with Jesus and I'm not letting that go.

Christianity isn't a mountain of do's and don'ts. It's a relationship and only God can help you find your balance and live your life to its fullest.

Day 19 - I'm Right, You're Wrong

But he gives more grace. That is why Scripture says: "God opposes the proud but gives grace to the humble,"

James 4:6

"What do you mean I'm wrong?" he asked. "Don't tell me I'm wrong! If anybody is wrong, it is you." Sound familiar? Proud people and/or those with poor self image usually rebel at any insinuation that they are less than perfect. Sometimes the response is teary with a statement of disappointment that you could possibly doubt their perfection. Other times the response is angry And almost always it is full of self-defense, focusing all blame away from themselves, or even denying the problem altogether.

I wish I could say this is a problem that has become extinct since James' time, but, unfortunately, I think it may have even grown in proportions. We have become so insecure that even the slightest reproof is taken as a personal attack. We are encouraged to be so in-touch with our feelings that emotion often controls our response, clouding or overwhelming the deeper issue of right and truth.

I once knew a man named Cove Marcum. Cove was a factory worker, but he also owned a farm where he raised some beef cattle. Cove also had horses and sometimes we would go over to his house and ride through the woods and trails around his house on a Sunday afternoon. Cove was a quiet man but very strong. I worked with him a couple of times at harvest season and was amazed at his strength. As I got to know him better, I became even more impressed with his spiritual strength. Although never loud or boisterous, people listened when he spoke. His concern was always for others and his life was obviously committed to Jesus Christ. Cove was one of the best men I ever knew. He was a living example to a generation of young people of what humility is really about. I know his example changed me.

Today's connotation of humility is wimpy and woebegone. Nothing could be further from the truth. True humility takes strength and heart. It is reflected in someone who stands for the right and yet doesn't demand that he is right. There is no ego problem for the humble person. James' quote here from Proverbs 3:31 points to the attitude approved by God.

Take a good look at how you respond to criticism and, without defending how you respond, see if your right is the only right you're willing to accept. If so, you're probably wondering "Where is God's Grace?" The answer is—it is going to someone else.

Day 20 – Warfare of a Different Kind

"Submit yourselves, then to God. Resist the devil, and he will flee from you."

James 4:7

This is a perfect set-up for a three part sermon. 1. Submit yourselves to God; 2. Resist the devil; 3. He will flee from you. This scripture is quoted often by those facing trials and tribulations with the intent to encourage the discouraged.

When asked how he was doing, my uncle Otis liked to respond with the phrase, "Fine as frog's hair split in two." This almost always got a smile and certainly, if taken literally, was descriptive of someone feeling in excellent. We often quote this passage from James 4:7 both to ourselves and to others without, I believe, any on-purpose application to our own lives. Even when we do apply it, it is usually quoted with the first part left out; you know, the part about submitting. Now, it's no secret that James was writing this book to supposed Christians. James discovered that we all need reminding from time-to-time of even the most elementary things and he hit the nail on the head. Submission to God is the beginning point of salvation when we acknowledge Jesus as Lord and Savior. Submission as a lifestyle is the essence of holiness and living out the sanctified life. One of my friends used to say, "Christians leak," meaning that we need to be constantly refilled with the Holy

Spirit and reminded of our walk with Him.

Not only does James remind us of who we are as Spirit-filled, submissive servants of the Lord, he commands that we resist the devil. It shouldn't have to be said! Sadly, practically, it does have to be said. Too many saints are dabbling around the edges of sin and temptation. Too many of us have begun to entertain arguments of our rights and privileges, rationalizing commerce with the devil.

True resistance means turning the television channel instead of watching shows, or even commercials, that incite lust and/or covetousness. True resistance means frequenting different stores when what is sold at one store means exposing ourselves to the pornographic or sensual.

True resistance means avoiding sexual innuendo, gossip, or flirtatious behavior at work, even when "everyone else is doing it." True resistance means doing the right thing even when everyone else is getting away with it. The devil is not always easy to resist. In fact, resistance usually costs us something. However, resistance always gains us something in our relationship with Him, not to mention the fact that it's kind of nice to see the devil running away.

Day 21 - Our Decisions Do Matter

"Submit yourselves, then, to God. Resist the devil, and he will flee from you. Come near to God and he will come near to you."

James 4:7, 8

It amazes me how make-up artists are able to totally alter the appearance of their subject. Satan has been using even more convincing disguises for thousands of years. His red suit and tail get-up only serves to draw attention away from his more subtle and devious disguises. Currently, there is an interest in "spiritual" things. Many books are being written about angels, crystals, channeling, etc. that might make the uninformed believe they have come into contact with God, when in reality their contact has been with Satan, in disguise. His greatest disguise is to present himself as an angel of light, and, as we all know, Jesus describes Himself as the light of the world.

The confusion which results has been successful in deluding many who are truly seeking the truth into believing a lie with all of its consequences (cf. Romans 6:23). Why do so many believe the lie? Because it is easier. Let's face it, Satan is intimately aware of the human condition. After all, it was his pride which got him where he is today. Because the devil knows us so well, he knows we want to be counted as righteous without too much effort and if we can rationalize some sin in the bargain, so much the better.

James says, "Resist the devil, and he will flee from you," and I believe that most of us would do this except we have trouble recognizing just what around us is "the devil." A simple test of basic Biblical knowledge of the foundational truths of God would immediately make it clear that there is a serious problem in America. George Barna, a popular analyst of religious trends in America, reports in *The Barna Report 1992-1993*, that only 8% of the population consistently responded to eight statements consistent with a Biblical perspective (p.56). The difficulty lies not in *resisting* but in *recognizing* the devil. Such recognition will only come through a more thorough knowledge of who God is as found in His Word. When we truly know

Him, it becomes easier and easier to recognize a phony.

"Oh, how I love your law!
I meditate on it all day long.
Your commands make me wiser than my enemies,
For they are ever with me.
I have more insight than all my teachers
For I meditate on your statutes.
I have more understanding than my elders,
For I obey your precepts.
I have kept my feet from every evil path
So that I might obey your word.
I have not departed from your laws,
For you yourself have taught me.
How sweet are your words to my taste,
Sweeter than honey to my mouth!

I gain understanding from your precepts;
Therefore I hate every wrong path.
Your word is a lamp to my feet
And a light for my path.
Psalm 119:97-05

Day 22 - A Read Do-Gooder

"Anyone, then, who knows the good he ought
to do and doesn't do it, sins."

James 4:17

Do you know the good you ought to do?
Probably you could spin together a
philosophical rationale for good in general,
and the pros and cons of doing good.
However, the real question is: What,
specifically, is the good you ought to do?
Narrowing the good down to such a focus
may mean your relationships with family,
friends, and enemies. It could apply to
your attention to the environment, or how
you cooperate with teachers, the law (e.g.
highway laws, tax laws, etc.), or social needs

of our day (e.g. homelessness). The tendency of our day is shuffle the good to somewhere low on our priority list. Other things, like looking out for number one, of course, must be pushed to the top. Our society continues to insist that our focus should be on ourselves and our needs and rights before any other consideration. This is a sure path to emptiness and eventual hopelessness. There is an obvious consequence in the verse from James: separation from God.

This separation is more significant and devastating to your soul's contentment than you know. You can see the effect of such hopelessness in the high incidence of teen suicide and the failing of America's moral strength. Popular jingles say "You deserve a break today" and "Have it your way." These messages mistakenly reinforce the concept that I am the center of my universe. It's time we listen and respond to James' admonition by going the way of that different drummer and do what is good, even if no one else does.

Day 23 - Wealth and Weeping

"Now listen, you rich people, weep and wail because of the misery that is coming upon you. ..."

James 5:1 (vs 1-6)

Obviously popularity was not a "virtue" sought after by James. Verses 1-6 would not be popular nor easily accepted by any people in any time. James' forceful comments almost seem like some sort of sour grapes comment, or bashing the rich because he isn't himself wealthy. If that is your reading of this, you would do well to stop and take another look. Money was one of the top subjects discussed by Jesus himself, and the use of personal resources is a clear indicator of allegiance. Over the years I have heard many different rationalizations for the expenditures considered extra. My favorite is, "Well, I don't have any other vices, so...." There is an unspoken assumption here that somehow everyone is entitled to at least one vice. Bizarre? No, simply a rationalization for satisfying ourselves.

Much of the churches of today fosters such a concept when preaching emphasizes a "name it and claim it" faith. Name the possessions you desire or the salary level you want in prayer, give financially to the church (a very important step), and you can claim the fulfillment of such visions. Of course, if your prayers don't come true, then perhaps your faith wasn't quite strong enough. Such preaching is an abomination before God. While God choses to bless some with more wealth than others, it is clear from James that He also requires more from them. Any life lived without the saving grace of Jesus Christ and the indwelling presence of the Holy Spirit is an empty and hollow existence, regardless of the richness of the trappings or the extent of the possessions; houses, boats, cars, cottages, jewelry, etc. Any life lived in the Spirit sees earthly resources as an avenue to assist others in need and point people to the good news of Jesus.

Someone has said that our checkbooks are a powerful theological statement. I think there is truth in that. Where is your allegiance? What is your goal? Where is the focus of your life?

Day 24 - Wealth, What is it Good For?

"Now listen, you rich people...Look! The wages you failed to pay the workmen who mowed your fields are crying out against you. The cries of the harvesters have reached the ears of the Lord Almighty. You have lived on earth in luxury and self-indulgence. You have fattened yourselves in the day of slaughter. You have condemned and murdered innocent men, who were not opposing you."

James 5:4-6

The community where I live is growing. New houses are being built at an amazing rate and what's more, they are expensive homes. The architecture is impressive, even down to the landscaping. I have heard that the mortgage payments on these homes can be so high that, although the home looks awesome on the outside, there aren't enough funds left to furnish the inside, which may be devoid of a stick of furniture. In most cases these homes are funded by two incomes, husband and wife, and occasionally the mortgage requires some overtime just to make the checkbook stay near the black.

I remember living in six different homes growing up; some were small, although the last was fairly good-sized. As I reflect back on each of those homes, it's easy to see how my parents were trying to provide the best for their family in each of those moves. Yet, what I remember most is not the quality or size of the home, but the love that was present. I remember the hugs and the picnics, the time of wrestling with

Dad and helping Mom. So, I think that with all the needs in the world today (e.g. homelessness, addictions, domestic violence, pornography, crime, etc.), maybe there's something to be said for the moderation of satisfying ourselves. Could it be that some of the resources we have tied up in our own pleasure should, in reality, go to meet the needs of others? All that we have, has been entrusted to us. Stewards or managers: when we are called to give an account, what will the verdict be?

Day 25 - I Am a Patient Person… Really!

"Be patient, then, brothers, until the Lord's coming. See how the farmer waits for the land to yield its valuable crop and how patient he is for the autumn and spring rains. You too, be patient and stand firm, because the Lord's coming is near."

James 5:7-8

I believe the Lord's return is near. The book of James was written approximately 1,800 years ago and he believed the Lord's coming was near. Aside from the controversy regarding the definition of "near" in eternal time spans, I think James expected to see Jesus return before he died. I, too, expect and hope for that day Jesus will return, and I pray that it happens soon. It could be that the Lord will return to take away the faithful in the next moment, or He might choose to wait for a few more years—or centuries—to pass. No one can accurately chart the day and hour of the Lord's return and those who say they can are only fooling themselves and those foolish enough to listen. Thus, whether or not the Lord's return is scheduled for today or next week, or next year, or next . . . , the point is not on the returning, but upon our *readiness* for that return.

This is where patience enters the picture. This is not the kind of patience required for a visit to the Department of Motor Vehicle. That kind of sitting and waiting until your number is called is as foreign to a true believer as a fish is to the desert. Our patience is urged, but other passages from the Word indicate that a sincere believer will be one who continues to diligently seek to do the will of the Father. That was Jesus' pattern until the day He was taken back into heaven and it should be ours. A true believer is not a pew-warmer who complains about this current generation, while doing nothing to enrich others. A true believer understands that time is short and has answered the call to share the good news with others before it is too late. This kind of patience is exciting and challenging, and worlds better than just sitting around, pretending to be religious...I mean patient.

Day 26 – Beware the Grumble Mumbles

"Don't grumble against each other, brothers, or you will be judged. The Judge is standing at the door!"

James 5:9

There are 18 references to grumble, grumblers, and grumbles in the New International Bible. Thirteen of those references are in the Old Testament. According to Webster's New Collegiate Dictionary, the word grumble means to "mutter in discontent." I just came back from a parents' meeting where there was some grumbling going on. Someone felt that another person's position was unreasonable, even though that position was legal. I noticed that the grumbling didn't do anything positive to resolve the situation; in fact the grumbling seemed to generate a negative atmosphere and more tension.

Grumbling is a symptom, like a cough or a runny nose. We treat symptoms and sometimes what is causing that symptom goes away. There are other times, however, when what is causing the symptoms not only doesn't go away, but actually gets worse. James admonishes the believers to not grumble against each other. This is good advice and may be taken as a spoonful of medicine and, if accompanied by prayer and attention to the Word, everything will be as it should be. However, if the symptoms worsen, some serious steps need to be taken.

In the case of grumbling, the underlying cause is always traceable back to a lack of trust and faith in God, as well as neglect of prayer and devotions. Some things can be fixed. In the case of the parents' meeting mentioned above, one person's decision forced the rest to become involved in seeking a new solution by working within the system. The point is clear, if something can be done, then do it. If there is nothing to be done or you are unwilling to use the energy (a common plight of our day) to overcome the problem, quit grumbling. If you are grumbling about how someone has treated you, do your best to resolve the issue and then *let it go*. Grumbling unchecked will embitter your soul and destroy your relationship with others and, eventually, with God. It doesn't take too many Old Testament examples to figure out that God isn't keen on grumblers.

Day 27 - Do You Finish What You Start?

"As you know, we consider blessed those who have persevered. You have heard of Job's perseverance and have seen what the Lord finally brought about. The Lord is full of compassion and mercy."

James 5:11

It is probably safe to say that every home in America contains a closet with unfinished projects. These projects range from those so simple they were given up out of boredom, or those so difficult that the return doesn't seem to match the investment of time and energy. Whatever the reason, there they sit, those unfinished projects. They aren't thrown out because we have somehow convinced ourselves that sometime (in the unforeseeable future) we are actually going to get around to finishing what we started. Nobody likes to be considered a quitter . . . so we simply put things on hold. This seems to carry over into the spiritual realm. Thus, we see those confessing to be Christians engaging in activities, relationships, or expressing attitudes that are clearly outside those outlined in the Word. We have so accepted our nature that we don't even notice the paradox.

At almost any marathon these days there are those whose sole purpose in running is to prove to themselves that they can finish. There is much to be said for the discipline required to finish. While those who finish after the others have gone home may not receive the prizes, they have the satisfaction of knowing they have persevered. Certainly, no prize would even be possible without that one qualification—actually finishing the race.

We need to re-examine our spiritual closet and see if, perhaps, we have not put aside the one relationship that is going to make an eternity's worth of difference. If we have found Christ either boring or too complex in the past, it might be time for a fresh start. Start by investing heavily, not of your finances, but of your heart. Give yourself 100% to the development of your relationship with Christ through prayer, reading of the Word, attendance at your church, and involvement in ministry. Someday may never come; it certainly won't for some of those leftover projects. Now is the time to get back in the race and persevere.

Day 28 - Everybody Has an "If" in Their life

"Is any one of you in trouble? He should pray. Is anyone happy? Let him sing songs of praise."
James 5:13

Note first of all that in both cases, trouble or happiness, the recommended response is directed at God. I know the first thing I want to do when faced with trouble is to sit down with pen and paper and try to figure out the pros and cons of the situation and attempt to develop an acceptable solution. I suppose that attempt at control is a leftover from the days before Christ became my Lord. It seems so obvious, yet prayer is so often pushed back or even forgotten in the face of trial or crisis.

Let me reiterate James' thought: If anyone of you is in trouble, pray. Pray that God will give you wisdom to know how to respond and what it is, if anything, you can do to resolve the problem. Pray that God will intervene and bring about a resolution. Pray and by faith, trust God.

Now when things are going well and we are happy, we seem to neglect or even forget God. Praises coming from our hearts and our lips acknowledge the fact that He *does* work all things together for the good of those who love Him and that He *does* give good gifts. It's never too late to begin praising God. Whether through songs of joy or words of praise, God loves it when He sees in us an attitude of gratitude. One of the great lacks of our day is that attitude of gratitude. Now that you have been reminded, what is there in your life right now for which you need to praise God? If you can't think of anything, then you better take the other route, and hit your knees in prayer!

Day 29 - Healing?!

"Is any one of you sick? He should call the elders of the church to pray over him and anoint him with oil in the name of the Lord. And the prayer offered in faith will make the sick person well; the Lord will raise him up. If he has sinned, he will be forgiven."

James 5:14,15

I still believe God heals. I belong to a denomination that has as one of its articles of faith the belief that God heals. Not only do I believe God heals, I have personally witnessed His healing. I have read and heard about other instances when God has healed miraculously. But, I am also aware of instances when God has not chosen to heal, or when the healing doesn't come on our timetable.

James says that if anyone is sick, he

should call the elders of the church to pray over him and anoint him with oil in the name of the Lord. This is a standard of the church that cannot be ignored, nor should it be. But it is also a subject which has caused much hurt and confusion for believers, particularly those who have attempted to follow James' directive and have not experienced healing. I know of some instances where individuals have simply been told they don't have sufficient faith to be healed, or that there is hidden sin in their life which is keeping them from being healed. This kind of response is similar to the advice Job received in the Old Testament as he was going through his trials. Sometimes there is truth in it, often there is not. The one who is ill now also must deal with the guilt, imposed by other "good" Christians, that they are somehow spiritually deficit as well as physically afflicted.

James says in verse 15: "And the prayer offered in faith will make the sick person well...." I would like to be able to assert that the reason there are not more healings is because those who are *praying* lack faith, not the person who is ill. I am certain that this is the case some of the time, but there are other times when the anointing and prayer is powerful with the presence of God, yet healing does not occur. Good people, people full of faith, die from diseases while other good people, and some not so good, are healed. I confess, I don't really understand why. I am convinced, however, that my lot lies with the three Hebrew children who responded to Nebuchadnezzar's threats of torture by saying, "O Nebuchadnezzar, we do not need to defend ourselves before you in this matter. If we are thrown into the blazing furnace, the God we serve is able to save us from it, and he will rescue us from your hand, O king. But even if he does not we want you to know, O king, that we will not serve your gods or worship the image of gold you have set up" (Daniel 3:16-18). Thus, I intend to follow James' advice and call upon the elders of the church and be anointed, but my trust is in God and whatever He decides is what I will ultimately accept.

Day 30 - Confession is Good for the Body and Soul

"Therefore confess your sins to each other and pray for each other so that you may be healed."
James 5:16a

James' conclusion comes on the heels of his directions for anointing and healing. In his concluding statement on the subject, he turns a corner and brings in a new thought: the confession of sins to each other as part of the healing process.

Confession of sins to someone other than God has long been a tradition of the Catholic church. Faithful Catholics have always been encouraged to participate in confession to their priest on a regular basis.

However, the Reformation brought a new view to the role of the priest and confession and the interaction between sinner and priest became a casualty as the Protestant church separated from its Catholic heritage. Without going into a deep theological discussion, most Protestant denominations designated confession as that which should be done between sinner and Christ, and that no other mediation is needed. I believe this to be true, however, I also believe there is power in James' conclusion for those who have ears to hear. Psychologists have long emphasized the emotional and even physical release to be found when one is able to unburden to another human who expresses genuine concern and interest. We were designed to exist in relationship with other human beings, and, while there are those who separate themselves from all human contact, it is a fact that relationships are the basis of life itself. I truly believe that if more of us would take the time to find and nurture a few strong relationships (I'm talking friends here) with people we could talk to and listen to, a significant number of counselors would have to close-up shop.

Think about it, then give it a try.

Day 31 - Prayer!

If there are only 30 days in the month, this devotional can be used in conjunction with the retreat schedule found at the end of the book

"The prayer of a righteous man is powerful and effective."

James 5:16b

I have had some prayers answered, and others not. When I say I have seen prayers answered, what I mean is that I have prayed and what I have asked to happen in prayer has transpired, sometimes in seemingly miraculous ways. When I say some of my prayers have not been answered, what I mean is that they were not answered as I *wanted* them to be answered. Interestingly, this passage is not about prayer being answered, which is what most of us think about when we think of prayer. Rather, James says that prayer can be powerful and effective . . . if prayed by a righteous man (person).

I want to start with the righteous man. A lot of people are praying today. In fact, thanks to the new age emphasis on spiritual things, there are probably more people praying today than ever before. There is, however, a small problem. The prayers neither originate with the righteous nor are some of them directed at the true God. All prayer is not equal. Prayers not directed at God are not prayers at all. It might be meditation, or yoga, or talking to yourself, or whatever, but it is not prayer. God might choose to act on such ramblings, but it is not prayer. When one emphatically insists that they are involved in prayer, but that prayer is not directed toward God the Creator, Jesus Christ, or Holy Spirit, what they are actually engaged in is idolatry, that is, the worship of idols. There is no question that there is much power and potential locked up in human beings. Sometimes, someone will happen across a way to unlock part of that potential and call that key "God." Unfortunately, many such keys are worshiped and prayed to with hearts sincere and full, only to discover the emptiness of their "god" at the end. It matters where the prayer is directed.

It also matters who is doing the praying. While it is clear from other passages that God always hears the prayer of confession from the lips of a sinner, James here points to the righteous man as having the "ear" of God. Unfortunately, many within the church have so overemphasized human perfection that we have begun to believe that James' promise is impossible for the average person to attain. Now, on the side of truth, the righteous *man* can easily and appropriately be translated righteous *person.* The big question is, how does one become righteous? I'm glad you asked. Righteousness is not earned, either through monetary gifts to God or the church, or through the practice of doing good things. Righteousness is *rooted* in faith in Jesus Christ and the Son of God and the acceptance of Him as Lord of our life.

Righteousness is the *response* of living in accordance with the commandment of love. Love the Lord your God with all of your heart, and all of your soul, and all of your strength and your neighbor as yourself. (Matthew 22:37-39) This is righteousness and when one lives like this, the prayer and the power just seem to happen.

Conclusion

I continue to see God's love striving in our hearts and the presence of good at work in our world.. Opportunities exist for us to live holy lives and stand for righteousness on a daily basis. The increased presence of technology in our world practically forces us to confront issues such as bioethics and personal priorities in the fast pace of our society. Values and morals that were constant only a generation or two ago are *constantly* being challenged and often discarded. Yet, here we are, precisely where God has placed us, with all the intelligence, will, and strength He knew we would need for the life we face. Will we make a difference? Is making a difference measured by some historically recorded accomplishment? Or, by a life changed and enriched because of our contact? How do you measure success? Does our involvement in justice by doing right, even in the face of temptation, qualify us to be called successful?

Holiness is a journey. Righteousness, faithfulness, love, mercy, goodness, and kindness are companions on that journey.

Bonus Retreat Section

A retreat away from the pressures of the challenges faced every day can provide a wealth of benefits. It can give new perspective, renewed vigor, renewed patience, and a deeper awareness of God's presence.

Here are some ways that your retreat experience will be most effective:

- Decide if you will be doing this retreat alone or with a small group of trusted friends. Probably no more than three. The key here is "trusted" as these individuals will be sharing and hearing you share some private thoughts.

- Decide on a space where you can remove yourself from contact with any part of your normal life. A park, a large library, a room in a church. If you use a church room, try to arrange to use one other than the one you normally attend as it will open up new experiences and better insure privacy.

- Eliminate cell phones and computers for this time.

- Fix a time between three and five hours, although this can be longer, the material here is designed around that time frame.

- Bring along your Bible in your favorite translation, this book and something to write in. The writing pad/tablet/journal will have many uses for the day such as making notes of stray ideas which might distract you so you can come back to them later, writing down observations from your times in prayer, answers to questions, and new insights from the Word or your discussions, if you have a small group.

- Consider whether you wish to fast as part of your experience. By that I mean skip a meal, either before, after, or during the retreat. Fasting can be a useful way to focus your thoughts and energies and is a practice employed by Christians from the earliest days. Even if fasting you should have water readily available.

If you are meeting in a small group, I have found that bringing the elements for communion can be a very effective ending to the retreat.

Retreat Schedule:

Begin with 30 minutes of quiet contemplation with just you and God. Even if you have a small group with you, this time should be spent alone.

Take the next block of time to worship God. Focus on nothing except worship. If you are with a small group, come together for this time of worship. For this you may want to use the hymnal/songbook you may have brought with you, or simply read from the psalms. Singing is a wonderful release of worship and is encouraged. The goal is to fully release yourself into a state of worship so don't be bound by time. This may take 15 minutes or 45 or longer.

Read the devotional below and answer the
questions posed at the end. If you have
come together as a small group, answer the
questions by yourself in silence first
(approximately 30 minutes) and then join
back together as a group and share
responses and challenge each other to
excellence (60 minutes).

Intervention...Through Me

"My brothers, if one of you should wander
from the truth and someone should bring him
back, remember this: Whoever turns a sinner
from the error of his way will save him from
death and cover over a multitude of sins."

James 5:19-20

What I see in this passage is that our lives
do make a difference. It does matter that

we exist. It does matter how we relate to those in our world. My involvement in your life may have eternal consequences. Unfortunately, my lack of involvement may also have eternal consequences. The mindset of our day is so focused on *me*, my rights, and what I deserve, that we easily rationalize our lack of involvement in redemptive relationships. Relationships that are redemptive include opportunities to be actively involved in turning a sinner from the error of his ways, as well as those which encourage fellow believers. "You deserve a break today," has so permeated our thinking that we have actually come to believe it. Isn't advertising wonderful?! The focus of this statement is all about ME and what I deserve. My "break" is interpreted in terms that benefit me, regardless of the needs of others. This philosophy runs contrary to the life and pattern Jesus left for us, "who, being in very nature God, did not consider equality with God something to be used to his own advantage; rather, he made himself nothing by taking the very nature of a servant, being made in human likeness. And being found in appearance as a man, he humbled himself by becoming obedient to death even death on a cross." (Philippians 2:6-8) So, following this example, pursue redemptive relationships, and by doing this you will adopt the mindset of Jesus Christ.

1. How have you personally fallen under the influence of the culture of "ME?"

What are the signs in your spending habits, your reading, your TV watching of this "ME" focus? What will you need to change in yourself to make redemptive relationships a central part of your life?

2. There are likely many individuals in your life who are not in a saving relationship with Jesus Christ. Take a few moments to consider these and then identify five for whom you will commit to praying for and influencing by your own life for their salvation.

3. There are individuals that are believers who are experiencing difficulties. The challenges they face may be so overwhelming that their faith is wavering. How can you come along

beside them to encourage and support them?   List at least three such individuals and your plan of support for each.

Following the devotional time spend the next 30 minutes again in silence alone. The goal of this time block is to allow the Holy Spirit to work through the day's experiences to reveal truth to your soul. It is not a time of petition, or even praise. It is a time of listening.

If you are alone on retreat finish the time by journaling your experiences and what you feel God has revealed to you. If you are in a small group this is still appropriate and encourage, however, you will benefit from ending your time together in communion. Sharing communion is the experience of sharing in the death and resurrection of Jesus Christ, and in the community of believers. In 1 Corinthians 11:23-26 Paul describes the communion ritual and that can be followed as you share the elements together.

Blessings,

Rick